Lo

Winner of the Iowa Poetry Prize

Lo

poems

Melissa Crowe

University of Iowa Press
Iowa City

University of Iowa Press, Iowa City 52242
Copyright © 2023 by Melissa Crowe
uipress.uiowa.edu
Printed in the United States of America
Design by Sara T. Sauers
Printed on acid-free paper

Library of Congress Cataloging-in-Publication Data
Names: Crowe, Melissa, author.
Title: Lo: Poems / by Melissa Crowe.
Description: Iowa City: University of Iowa Press, [2023] |
    Series: Iowa Poetry Prize
Identifiers: LCCN 2022042711 (print) | LCCN 2022042712 (ebook) |
    ISBN 9781609388997 (paperback) | ISBN 9781609389000 (ebook)
Subjects: LCGFT: Poetry.
Classification: LCC PS3603.R689 L6 2023 (print) |
    LCC PS3603.R689 (ebook) | DDC 811/.6—dc23/eng/20220909
LC record available at https://lccn.loc.gov/2022042711
LC ebook record available at https://lccn.loc.gov/2022042712

Contents

The Self Says, I Am

The heart says, I am less;
The spirit says, I am nothing.
—THEODORE ROETHKE

Say I'm clover and Queen Anne's
lace, devil's paintbrush and lupine.
I'm a yard of junked cars, each
with its corona of broken glass

and never-mowed grass. Dirt trail
to cattail. My heart this sudden
pond, this skipped stone. Say
I'm a girl in a sundress, perpetual

beginner in a cloud of bees
and blackflies and my heart a foraged
apple, still green. Say, *O my bones,*
my heart's a whiskey bottle

glinting from the weeds. I pull
a wagonload of hearts to the store
at the end of my road, trade them
for dimes, and say the dimes

become my heart. They call this
redemption. I'm the field of goldenrod
behind the empty chicken house.
My heart's a span of wasted sheet metal

that burns there noondays, blisters
feet. Near suppertime, my heart's
the leaf that volunteers in the shade
of the woodshed. It tastes of lemon

and is safe to chew. Then my heart's
a bowl of poor man's stew, salt broth
and slivers of meat. By bedtime
I'm *a learned, nimble girl,* sunburned

and yearning before the box fan.
My heart the mosquito coil, the bugs
blooddrunk. My heart the dishrag
dipped in vinegar. The hand

that soothes. The meager breeze.
The heat. *Before the moon draws back,
dare I blaze like a tree?* What if I'm
this body, TV blue and sweating

on a blanket of stiff wool,
and my heart's an old, sad dog,
stretched out beside me?
What can I tell my bones?

Before they're stones under stones,
tell them the French words for summer,
hunger, choice. That the nothing
echoing the culvert is my voice.

·I·

Thrownness

Remember burdock, hooked in clusters to the cable knit
of your dingy white tights, fall afternoons when you
walked home through backyards, waist-high fields?

Or the pitch that marked your fingers, first with its own
amber glue, then with everything you touched: pollen,
dog hair, dirt. Maybe home is what gets on you and can't

be shaken loose. Remember armyworms? Your grandfather
ringed the base of each tree with foil, and still those
caterpillars ate through all the leaves, a devastation

in steadfast, wriggling lines. They swarmed the streets,
and, riding your bike, you avoided their bodies
until you didn't, until you'd absorbed enough

of Grampy's ire, his anxiety, and training your front tire,
surprised the hot top with their glossy yellow blood,
same tar you scraped yourself across, afternoons

you wobbled from your skates or, breaking hard,
hurled over handlebars, the skin sheared from your knees
and palms so your own familiar blood revealed itself

again. Maybe home is what gets in you, until you're made
of nothing but its stuff. Remember how your street
was flanked by two men's houses, one a trailer like a tin can

but filled somehow with sunshine even winters, all its rough
surfaces blessed by the washrag of the busy old gentleman
who gave you chocolate kisses and wanted—you'd still

swear—nothing in return. Remember how every branch
on that same street seemed blessed with fat red berries
your mother said would make you sick and how—always

hungry, cupboards bare—you would not stop tasting them
anyway. How could the fruit of every bush be poison?
How could something that looked so sweet deliver

such bitterness to your tongue? That sick taste threatened
to convince you such reversals of fortune were the only
kind you'd know, though asked just what and where

you meant to be when you grew up you said an actress,
artist, astronaut, the moon. Maybe home is cargo
you can't put down? In any case, the other man's

house, with its friendly front door and backyard pool,
became the darkest cave, and so you slid into
the gravel pit, where—in an effort to preserve your faith—

you used your two thin arms to raise above your head
rocks as fat and dull as trout bellies, then loosed them
so they fell against the shale below and split. On TV

you'd seen the otherworldly geode, dry fist of shit
that opened onto secret glowing facets, such sudden
purples as you might feel called to pray to, so you knew

a thing like this could look less blessed than it was, skidded
on your ass into that hole and shattered rock after rock,
believing some rare marrow might reveal itself to you,

some strange, some unexpected source of light. But no.
Everything you managed to open in that low place
was nothing but itself the whole way through.

I'm Not Mad at My Mother for Letting Me Roam the Neighborhood Unsupervised

She told me her girlhood's a ghost—so translucent,
so near gone reminiscing's like waving her fingers
through smoke. Last week she texted me a photo
her cousin texted her: classroom full of children,
bright faced at their desks. It's me, she said. Aren't I
cute? And she was. I thought to ask, Do you
remember? But she seemed so happy just to be told
this smile was hers on a day she lived, just to learn
those were her cheeks, her hair so neatly combed,
looked like somebody who loved her had done up
the many buttons on her dress. It's true that parts
of little-girl me are solid. Every place, for instance,
that she ran her finger over I can touch, soft circuit
around my mouth and nose, each little eyebrow like
smoothing the burrs on a stalk of Timothy weed,
which is another thing I remember—walking everywhere
with her, the laundromat, the store, on pavement, sure,
but oftener through backyards, pine woods, how I'd
crouch to disappear in weedy ditches and she'd pretend
panic, then joy when I leapt into sight. It's also true
that sometimes I was nowhere she could see, in my own
woods or wandering the old airport with its cracked
tarmac and shattered windshields. Some days
she didn't know where I was, which was okay except
when it wasn't. I don't know what thief stole my mother's
past. I don't even wish I did, can't tell if it'd be a kindness
or a sin to say to her that parts of my girlhood, too,
are gone, but suddenly I recall that if I lay on my back
on that abandoned runway, I could see planes take off
from the new airport nearby. I didn't imagine myself
a passenger, not exactly, as those big bodies
flew over mine, welcome terror, obliterating glee.

When I Was Afraid

The bear in the room every night. Because bears somewhere, bears
everywhere. Bear in the room because bears in the world, because
if it can happen, it is. Happening. His feral bulk somehow
in the house—no, not somehow because I know how, read
an article about a bear busting a screen off a bathroom window,
climbing through. The bear in the room because one bear
somewhere one time busted through, looking for food.
Was in a room. Was hungry enough. This bear hungry, too? All
bears everywhere hungry. All hungry bears in the room.
Their claws. Their teeth. Their unknowable intentions. No,
I know their intentions—my father told me the story of a man
mauled in daylight on a soccer field. That bear mauling means
this bear in my bedroom means to maul me. All mauling bears in
my bedroom, on their hind legs. Because one time. Because bears.

But Nothing Bad Ever Happened to Me in the Woods

where there were never any men just cousins
and dogs and rubber dolls and birdchatter
and razor-cut light and trails of scat I could
subject to scansion figure out whose feet
I followed through leaf litter rabbits rabbits
deer never any bears but always thick as musk
the promise of bears who kept their distance
our hollering having preceded us
to the blackberry patch where we stained our
thieving mouths our bellies our hands because
we could because we could not help it
where once we built a plywood boat
rough platform set upon a row of tires
so we wobbled the deck when we walked it
like the sea might roll beneath sailors in a storm
might toss unwatched children to their deaths
danger we welcomed we made and so constrained
where in winter we skated skateless through
an ice-slicked clearing no fathoms beneath
and where in warmer months we waded
the creek its surface delicately pocked
by legs of water bugs its cold music on bare
skin a good surprise where the plot
never sickened and when late afternoon began
its early forest darkening we'd find our way slowly
and adroitly back to neighborhood and day
but first we built floorplans of pine straw
grids of little rooms in which we pretended eating
from the broadleaf plates we heaped with weeds
and cones and seeds as though to sup were
up to children simple as to chat or sing an airy
consequenceless thing feat we could do here
or maybe—easy as to drink or fight—anywhere.

Epithalamium with Paper Bell

I was there on the day my mother married—
I've seen photographs of her in her borrowed
dress, bodice of a taller friend wrinkled
at her waist, slack satin pooling at her feet.

Her forehead shines above a startled smile,
and my sudden stepfather, in a rented tux
of powder blue, just looks glad. There I am,
too, tucked between them on my final

day of being five years old. I don't remember
the ceremony or the reception, the kind I'd
later love when my mother's younger brothers
wed their first or second wives at the Elks Club

or the VFW, center of the room cleared
for a dance floor, tables pushed to the walls
and spread with crockpots of cabbage rolls,
spam salad spooned into hot dog buns.

Beer bottles and ashtrays. Uncles with their
sleeves rolled up, Red Wings buffed of mud.
When they weren't twirling girlfriends
with spaghetti straps and long-long hair,

pulling them close for the slow tunes,
they lifted me into their arms so I could hug
their whiskered necks. There'd have been
a deejay and gallons of milk mixed with Kahlua,

a dollar dance, man after man paying to twirl
my mother a little, money for the honeymoon,
one night in a cabin on Portage Lake then back
to the shoe factory. But I only remember

the paper bell I found taped to a table that night,
miracle the way I could close its feathers so
easily, conceal the whole voluminous thing
between two half-bells of card, then open it

as swiftly as lungs can fill with breath.
Like hands that part to reveal what I'd
wished for bent at the bedside, what I'd seen
in my head and whispered into the dark.

I could almost have believed I heard it ringing,
that tissue bell, marvelous flat nothing
come to song. I kept it a long time, precious—
and then I guess I lost it. I guess we all did.

I Want to Tell You What Poverty Gave Me—

a life outside capital, though I know it doesn't
seem to make sense, given my grandfather's knuckles,
cold-cracked and smelling always of kerosene,
my uncle's back permanently bent in the shape

it took to lay two decades' worth of brick.
Or afternoons spent shaking down sofas
and chairs, fingers slid between car seat
and console, seeking coins for a hot dog

at Susan's Market or a pack of my mama's
Merit Menthols or to pay the paperboy,
sometimes somebody's father who needed
the money, too. Maybe the early bus to subsidy

breakfast, first time I saw yogurt, heaping pans
of the stuff, that sweet, pale purple spooned
into its compartment on my tray next to a little
box of some cereal we couldn't get with vouchers,

Frosted Flakes or Fruity Pebbles, and my choice
of peanut butter gone warm and soft or a single
melted slice of cheese like a slick of cartoon
sunshine on white toast. Fresh delights I paid for

only in shame. And look—a line of rocks plucked
from the nearest ditch showed twelve shades
of earth from gray to pink, and Nana said
the one ringed with a stripe of quartz was a wish—

lucky, like the park with its pondful of tadpoles
or the library's shelf of mangled pop-up books
nobody could check out but anybody could touch,
flat paper and then—turn the page or pull the tab—

a world. Maybe it was Gram bringing me things
she found in the hotel rooms she cleaned:
transistor radio, abridged copy of *Kidnapped*,
and once a waist-high bowling trophy, me winning,

no matter whose name was etched in the plate.
Or maybe the way we ran a hot bath only once,
and together my mother and I dulled its sheen
with Ivory suds, our dirt, before my father lowered

himself into the gone-cool water, how this
necessary sharing somehow welcomed me nightly
to the difficult world. Maybe my mother holding
my hand while we, carless, walked through near-dusk

blizzard from our place on one side of town
to her brother's in low-income on the other,
so we were swallowed and swallowed as we moved
through undifferentiated space, no knowing

whether the ground beneath us was front yard
or sidewalk or street, and when we arrived
in the warm somewhere of my uncle's apartment—
which might have been floating in the ocean

or moored on the dark side of the moon, judging
by the blackened windows and the scarcely muted,
cosmic howl of the storm—the local news was on,
and there we were, I swear it, in the weather report,

my mother in her old blue coat, and hidden
under mine, I knew, was a chain of red crochet
she'd made to join my mittens so they wouldn't
be lost, and if in that vast wildness we were

so tiny we could barely make out the specks
of ourselves, what was this wealth? Practically
fractal, nearly out-of-body. In this moment lifted
from time, we were famous to ourselves, beings

in the world not once, but look—twice, so who
knew, who knew how many times we could appear
or where? Maybe that was the winter we lived
in a rental without a working refrigerator, cartons

of milk lodged in the snow outside the front door,
the stuff always a little frozen when we drank it,
those crystals too a magic we made because we could,
because we had to. I even ate the snow, in a big bowl

with Kool-Aid, scrappy sub for the Slush Puppies
I'd yearn for come summer, pick bottles to buy.
And here I am talking again about buying things,
but what I hoped you'd see is that so often—

for stretches of days—we didn't. Couldn't. *Free.*

·II·

Poet Loves Hunter Though She'll Eat No Meat

No way to hear the word *merganser*
and not think about my father
who spoke it so tenderly, by which
I mean precisely, just the way
he schooled his retriever to hold
the bird itself—in a *soft mouth*—to prevent
the dog developing a taste for flesh.
Once he gave me the wing of a partridge,
bit of gristle at the hinge still tinged
with dried blood, and when you palmed
that silken thing and pressed its knob
of cartilage, it opened—splay
of dun-colored feathers—as if to fly.
And somewhere in memory, too, I hold
rabbit's foot after rabbit's foot (though
my father did not like to hunt them,
said when shot they cried like babies,
made him sad), not the garish
dime-store kind my friends hung
from their backpacks by a link
of chain, dyed cherry red or shocking
pink, just the soft pale fur, no copper
cap to hide the bone, which jutted
sharp right where it had been broken
off. That's not the part I rubbed
between my finger and my thumb
but might have tongued it once—
best way to know a thing's to taste it.

Lo

At the bible camp there were horses, massive hay-smelling
beasts I couldn't ride without the fiver for the upcharge.
At the horse camp, lo, there were bibles, free, green leatherette
with uncracked spines and I'd soon cracked mine, with a marker
lit each begat, every revelation, then held the wild thing closed
during night church, touching its sticker, wiggle-eyed lion
with a speech bubble that read, *I'm a King's kid*. Afterward
in the deeper dark of the cabin, crowded with three-story bunks,
so many girls praying then asleep above me, I wrote on myself
with my finger, *When I wake, I will be satisfied*, but next morning
stood longing in the sawdust of the barn where the horses ambled
out of reach and perched in every saddle a girl with bare legs
and boots, straddling. Later when Pastor Steve in his cowboy hat
and pearl-button shirt waved the good book and said, *Raise
your hand if you haven't yet been saved*, my arm shot up though
I'd been saved and saved: year before at Calvary Baptist,
year before that at Vacation Bible School where I'd won a golden
lapel pin—JESUS LOVES ME—for memorizing more psalms
than anybody: *He maketh me to lie down in green pastures.
Our bodies cling to the ground*. Still I climbed the steps to join him
on the stage, say yes again to God. I'd be a King's kid, goddamnit,
confess enough times to finally make it stick, feel the grace
I glimpsed on the pastor's scrubbed-clean face. *I will not violate
my covenant or alter what my lips have said*. At the bible camp,
at the horse camp, breath huffed from velvet snouts rose, and, lo,
sweet breath from girls' slack mouths gathered at the ridge beam
and maybe slipped through. My breath, too. Sure as I pressed
hot hands together, asked the silence for what on waking nights
I think I still might want: to be lifted from my life by some
animal bigger than me. Possessed of lungs, wet eyes, silken
flanks, I burn. Lowing, lo—feet in sawdust, head upturned.

I'll Tell You What Helped

Listening to "Billie Jean" in my shag-carpeted bedroom,
combing and combing Barbie's crimped hair, all that perfect,
plastic silk. Sliding her in and out of her pink gown,

her canopy bed. And crying helplessly after the girl down the hall
(who I'd kissed the night before in the field of milkweed behind
our building with my hand between our mouths, our bodies so

neatly aligned) brought her mother to the door to tell mine
I'd said the f-word on the bus—*a lie,* howling out that grief
and then my mother believing me. Staying home sick the next day

to watch *3-2-1 Contact,* eat cold pork chops under an afghan
on the couch. My mother believing me. Mr. Rogers' slow,
coaxing timbre, his insistence on the existence of beauty

inside. To see him sprinkle the water above the goldfish
with flakes that drew them with a swiftness almost too instant
to believe. Their yearning, that relief. Then the Bloodhound Gang,

all rangy limbs and tennis shoes and sweatbands, getting
to the bottom of things. Afternoons spent marking the grayish
paperback pages of Judy Blume with Cheetos fingerprints

and practicing the recorder, its unsteady music like the mournful
breaths of an animal I thought I knew. My classmate Kelly's
ribboned coil of hair, her piano hands. Watching her strange

smart mouth move while she talked about her aching love
of the dog she couldn't have because of her sister's asthma.
So well I understood this longing (for some persistent warmth,

some trusted muzzle, creature with teeth, sure, but it won't ever
bite me) my adoration persevered even after she said, sorrowful
but resolute, that if faced with the choice to save a dog or me

from a burning building, she'd choose the dog—not her dog
(which, see above, she didn't have) but Any. Dog. At. All.
It helped to love her. I'm saying it hurt to love her, but I did.

Often in Dreams She Was My Girlfriend Until I Remembered, Still Asleep, That It Wasn't Okay

Her hair was a miracle of brown-black curls,
spring coiled and shiny, and she sprayed it
with TRESemmé and hung it over the edge
of the bed while she slept on slumber-party
Saturday nights so she wouldn't have to
wash it before church, and six birthmarks
half a shade darker than the rest of her creamy
olive skin traced her cheek from one earlobe
to the corner of her mouth. At video dances,
held tight to the stiffening groin of my own
partner, I watched her unfocused eyes
and bored frown while a punk kid, thick chain
padlocked around his neck, nuzzled hers.
Did she like it? I couldn't tell, but when they
broke up, he carved her name into his chest
with the point of his knife. I still think of how
those letters, crooked and keloid, must mark him
after all these years. She introduced me,
kid from a canned fruit cocktail family,
to the pomegranate, its pressed paper rind,
those nestled ruby cells, each with a seed
that nearly filled it. So many tiny morsels
and so much work to get their meager juice.
But sweet enough to make it worth it. To stain
my hands, my face, my precious white cotton
leggings with the delicate cuff of lace at each ankle.
On a night when we'd driven three hours south
to walk the strange, thrilling circuit of the nearest
shopping mall (Orange Julius! The Gap!), we lay
on our stiff-sheeted hotel bed in our tank tops
and underwear, facing each other in the dark,
and she asked me if I'd ever thought about
kissing a girl. I said yes. Then we stayed silent
and still until morning, neither of us rolling over
to get comfortable or adjusting our hard pillows
or hanging our hair over the bed's edge
to keep it neat. I could hardly hear her breathe.

Monachopsis Aubade

I don't want to stay folded anywhere,
because where I am folded, there I am a lie.
—RAINER MARIA RILKE

Once I slid into a one-man tent with a boy
I thought I wanted, lay all night breathing

his breath and woke cured of desire, so
filled was I with exhalation, his wet molecules.

For breakfast I ate my first satsuma
and, by his example, pocketed pith and peel

so as not to convert bears to desire
for a sweetness they'd have to steal from us.

Mosquitoes sucked and swelled me because
the bug spray I'd brought, he said, was poison,

and I didn't brush my teeth because where
would I spit the poison foam, obviously not

on the ground. I thought my mother
might die while we traipsed the woods

that weekend—she lay post-surgery
in a down-state hospital, my father

wetting her lips with a pink sponge
on a stick—but I didn't say so. On Sunday,

afloat in a quarry of bracing water so deep
I couldn't see bottom, I watched the young

men dive. Their bodies seemed clumsy,
however muscled and lithe, between their legs

that slack sex. I watched the women too,
baring their sunburned breasts. Then in my

t-shirt and knee-length shorts, I climbed
from the quarry and my left foot pressed

a ledge littered with broken glass that sliced
my instep so I hobbled the hike home in that

boy's wake and knew I wanted something
else, not this or him but, please, a thing

unfolding, that sometimes lets me lead
and leaves me hungry though I eat and eat.

Lessons

for Mark

At four I learned from my uncle's forearm split wrist to elbow &
leaking blood on Formica tabletop & linoleum floor that strangers
in dive bars—or on the very streets I walked in daylight with my
mother to the grocery store or park—will cut you. Eight years old
I learned from uncle's drunken cries & how he pounded fists
against his pickup that a brother can break your heart & from that
brother I learned there are things you'll steal even from people
you love if you want them bad enough. At twelve I learned from
my aunt wrenching child from husband & toward her lover's car
that bitterness binds us sometimes surer than love, the distinction
blurred in a boozy driveway, their firstborn dead three summers
& Tom Petty's gritty croon an eight-track soundtrack pouring
from lover's rolled down window & he doesn't get out. Just sits
with his sunburned arm flicking ash on the pavement like he's
got all night to wait. I was sixteen when I learned my grandfather
could no longer tell me from my mother or that year from 1975—
Sandy he kept saying *that bitch sat on the shed roof waving
a whisky bottle and laughing while they buried my mother* &
by *bitch* he meant my Gram from whom I'd learned men are hooks
I shouldn't let into me & that it's okay to sleep alone without
drawers on under my nightdress. At seventeen I learned no house
is emptier than one you've begged to be left in while your father
takes your mother south again to have the cancer out hopefully
but definitely her uterus & whatever else they find eaten by the
stuff that made her bleed so much on the bed the mattress couldn't
be saved. Even with the dog in the yard I didn't feel as brave as
I thought I would & though I could see my grandfather's house
from the porch of my own I didn't go there where I'd be called
by the wrong name. Instead I called you & you came as you always
did & as you still do—with a carton of Five Alive & a fistful
of daisies & you said *Melissa, Melissa* & I let you in. I let in
whatever that might bring & you touched me in ways that made me
forget—want to forget—every single other thing I'd ever learned.

·III·

III

When She Speaks of the Fire

she has to turn from it, so the story you hear
is that of pines and twitching leaves
and how her body is like neither—
—KATIE FORD

I didn't know the term then—cul-de-sac—
    just knew at the bottom of its belly
spread a permanent yard sale, old handsy
    man with a greasy gaze who priced
his bait (ceramic cats and china dolls
    and tin kazoos) so high I couldn't buy
anything. On either side lived girls
    from my school, pink cheeks
and Aqua-Netted hair. Girls on skates who rolled
    down the throat of that street. Now
when we meet, their memories are
    different from mine. One says, these years
later, *I knew better than to go there*. Fine.

Wired to forgive and to beg forbearance,
to mistrust my own intentions, I lay still
in my narrow bed and asked God to spare
every soul I knew from the poison
thoughts that might escape my head
and sicken them. *To imagine* the same
as *to curse*, anyone for whom I failed
to ask the Lord's protection
struck down the next day, so my prayers
could last all night: don't let Mama's cancer
come back, Lord; don't let there be razors
in my sister's candy apple; Lord, spare us
annihilation should the Russians finally
drop their bombs on Loring AFB. Let my
parents find out, don't let my parents
find out about the man, the man's hands.
And having heard them joke about *spontaneous
combustion*, I prayed, Dear Jesus, don't let
that sudden fire burn in me.

There's what happened in the bedroom
into which my friend's father carried me
on the day of the pool party, but what

happened before we cleared its threshold
(fingers slid beneath the loose crotch
of my suit) is the only thing I know I know.

I also know when that man's face appeared
on our TV three years later—family gathering,

mother, grandmother, aunts making
cabbage rolls in the galley kitchen, within

earshot of the local news, or bringing
my uncle a beer, their fingers greased

with hamburger meat, a smear still on
the bottle in my uncle's hand—everyone

recognized him, our old neighbor, so-and-so's
father, bus driver for the training center,

aboveground pool in his backyard summers,
and winters he flooded a patch of shoveled

lawn and built a skating rink, set up karaoke
in his garage, a stage and wired mics

for the neighborhood kids to sing
Kenny Loggins, the soundtrack to *Footloose*

all the rage that year. They could see his
mugshot, those women who loved me.

They could hear he'd been arrested for
molesting the kids he drove to school.

Upstairs in my room was the small guitar
my parents had given him permission

to give me. Thank god I thought, burning,
somebody will ask me. Nobody asked me.

Thank god I thought, burning, knowing
for the first time maybe what he'd

done to me, that what he'd done to me was
wrong enough to go to jail for, if you told.

Nobody asked me. I understood they knew
already. I understood they didn't want to know.

I read animals can sense any disaster
that's natural—smelling wildfire, they run
or stand in water or hide under rocks
or bury themselves in the dirt. Some die

in the flames, the very old, the young,
but most survive to starve or wander,
homeless, into cities, dangers their noses
can't detect—aftereffects more deadly

than the blaze itself—so when a hand
sets fire to the woods, it incinerates a day
and suffocates a future. I'm saying
the arsonist's a villain—this villainy

the kind we have to breathe: it fills the air,
our lungs, with choking smoke for miles,
for weeks. But when they asked *why*
of the man who, with a flick of his wrist,

lit up the Nantahala National Forest
and he said he just wanted to see something
burn? I didn't hate him. I'd been engaged
in such long calibration, careful how much

heat to release. Careful not to speak what I
wouldn't like to hear myself say. But words
inside a body can ricochet—maybe you've
felt it, too. Listen, I'm afraid of matches.

Nobody had to warn me not to play with fire.
My uncles burned garbage, didn't they?
I thought maybe that man had swallowed
so much rage everything to him was garbage.

And what about me? Girl to whom language
seemed an element so reactive it wanted only
my breath to ignite it, each word a sliver
of phosphorous I held in the dark of my mouth.

the most dangerous (they didn't)
     moment comes when a window
          breaks (ask me)   air sucked
    into the airless

space   a helpless (they didn't ask me)
     respiration   sudden
          involuntary breath
    before the room gone

still and silent   reignites   my chest
     hurts when I
          imagine giving you this
    story   it hurts when I

keep it to myself   you know (they didn't
     ask me) what I want? I want
          to have nothing
    to tell   or for everyone

who lodged a cinder in any
     kid's throat to go
          to hell (they didn't)
    the only thing worth saying

maybe? (ask me) *this body*
     wasn't for you (they didn't
          ask me) *this body isn't*
    for you   but friend, can you (they didn't)

forgive me if I'm still (ask me)
     not sure what good saying it
          can do   what harm saying (they
    didn't ask me) will do?

One uncle said her tits looked
nice in her sweater, told her

to twirl in her skirt. One uncle
laughed, muscling the cousins

into his massive arms where they
dangled, bodies pressed together

till they cried. When one uncle
visited, he wore gym shorts without

underwear, sat in the easy chair,
his leg over its arm, cock and balls

displayed for her between slack
cotton and hairy thigh.

In the night kitchen, one uncle
held a gun to the head of one

girl's mother, slit the kitten's
throat. Two uncles one latchkey

day made their way into the
house, the bedroom. One uncle

held the closet door closed
on her brother while the other—

I'm afraid to tell you the rest, afraid also
to leave you on that em dash forever,
watching through a crack as thick as a man's
fingers what unfolds beyond your power
to undo. Maybe you've been trapped these
long years, too. Of course, any house can be
a closet, the mind can be a closet, and some
basement-nautilus-jacked arm, some world-
harmed, harming clown still bars the door.

When I was four, an older kid
    had a playhouse, windowless
plywood walls and a rough-cut door

    with a padlock on the outside.
(It was a shed, not a playhouse at all,
    that's just what he called it,

the way the mugshot man would later
    call *a pool* the plastic muckhole in which
he lurked below the surface wearing

    goggles.) There I was lured and locked
in—we were *playing house*, but an hour
    passed in that splintery dark before

I knew the game was different
    and cried out. I can't remember
rescue or escape, whether the boy

    returned or my mother
heard my panic and her face appeared
    in a widening crack of light.

I say this to myself to save
myself: *You were right.*
They didn't want to know.
And you were smart to grasp
the way the elders turned
their backs, returned to their
crockpots, spread the meal
before you, whose eyes they
could or would not meet.
Maybe some of them choked
on what they tried to swallow,
swallowed what they might
have said. But to stay free
don't we have to call a hole
a hole, a goddamn shed a shed?

In wild fantasies I use my own

two feet to kick that flimsy

door apart—I can smell its rotting

wood and feel the sweat that wet

my back. In even wilder fantasies

I burn it to the ground, sometimes

after, sometimes before I'm found.

My good husband—he was

screaming, too, from a closet,

in the clutch. He's out here now

with me, we're both alive. We touch.

·IV·

VI

Epithalamium with Inventory

I had a moon—did you?—and a sky
to keep it in and a forest wide as night
and winking with eyes. I had mornings—
did you have mornings?—and a sun

to sweeten them and on a wire
out the window oil-purple crows,
their dry throats cracking me awake.
I had a bus with a driver named Charlie,

torn green seats and a kinder-racket
to convey me toward the day.
I had a town through dirty glass—
and you?—drugstore, post office, a river

wrinkled with light. Sudden school,
its hot top and jungle gym, knees bleeding
through tights, bloody tights, yes,
and an ache to go home but the bell rang,

I had a bell, a bright rough music in air,
in my chest. I had a chest, you had a chest—
I know it—with fist inside, clenching.
Did you have a blackboard and a woman's

hand, bone-white chalk drawing a world
then erasing, drawing and erasing,
palimpsest of ghost-worlds without cease?
I had lined paper and a fat blue pencil,

dominant hand and an edict not
to use it, clumsy otherhand they said
I should. I did. I had a name I wrote
backward—and you? You had a name,

but I couldn't call it, and a hand, two hands
I'd not yet held. We each had a house key,
didn't we, empty apartment and afternoons
yawning like holes, and I had a neighbor

hard in his ways like the pit I mistook
for a mine and slid into, each of its gems
just a lump of dull earth. I climbed out.
You climbed out. Did I have a mother?

If I had a mother, you did, too, and fathers?
We must have had them, yes, teachers
and fathers, buses and moons. Days
like smoke or like cool ether we breathed

and breathed through, and what do I have
now? O moon, o day, window, river,
blood, o bird, o hand, o fist, o world—
you. And will you have me, too?

The Parting

What hurt me so terribly
all my life until this moment?
—JANE KENYON

Husband, I didn't know the beautiful
broad-winged shape riding the air above us
as we lay in the hammock under the loblolly

pines was a buzzard until you told me.
Namer of whatever dark thing hovers,
you too deserve the truth, so when the police

find your father in a slick of blood
and offer no explanation but *natural causes,*
I say he drank himself to death, thinned

and thinned the skin of his esophagus
until it split. There's a word in Japanese
we can't translate though we take a sentence

to try: *This is the parting.* Singular goodbye
or something like an endless taking leave.
You nightwalked the frozen river between

your house and mine those years ago, believing
breakage as likely as love. Still a boy, you'd
already reckoned with your slide into the airless

place beneath this place—but I didn't know it.
Today, sad again to the point of rage, you say
I'm ready to go. The truth is, even I'm getting

close. We're stepping onto ghost glass together
or spooning under talons, some hungry beast.
Not always guests at the feast. *The parting,*

I might have said, sixteen, holding your electric
hand in movie-theater dark or marrying you under
leaf-cut sky or convulsing beneath your loving,

helpless gaze, our child wrecking through me
into life. Last night I shuddered above you, then—
This is the parting—lay laughing beside you

in our bed. I won't say *stay* because you won't
say you will. If I'm lucky, if I'm brave, we'll keep
birthing an ending into ravening light.

After Not Having Spoken to His Father for Fifteen Years, He Authorizes the Cremation

We must receive the body
in a casket leak-proof
and combustible with metal
handles to be retrieved
by magnet after burning.
We reserve the right
to reserve what we pull
from the ash in this way:
gold teeth, bridgework,
bullets. After a cooling
off period we rake what
we can from the chamber
but understand some remains
remain unrecoverable,
some bones won't burn
but must be pulverized,
ground to powder
and added to the urn.
Understand despite our
efforts some particles
may comingle with
those of others burned
in the chamber before
so that when all is said
and done we relinquish
to you a Decedent both
more and less than himself.

After Having Declined to Attend the Memorial Service, He Reads
the Messages Left by Mourners on the Funeral Home's Website and
Speaks His Own Elegy to the Photograph of His Father on the Screen

Dear Dad, you shouldered your burden
a long time. I'm sorry I couldn't help
you carry it. You can put it down now.

Poem Written after I Have Again
Needlessly Hurt My Husband's Feelings

He keeps seeding a body-sized
patch of ground bare of grass
in our front yard, carrying home
sacks of the stuff, mixed with
fertilizer and mulch, watering
the dirt morning and evening
with a plastic can, believing
the force of the hose might be
too much. Lovingly. Tenderly.
Through the window I can see
his broad back, a view I adore
above all others save his face.
You know the moment
the beloved, through a crowd
of strangers, reappears, moving
toward you? That. That's my
favorite scene to watch.
But I'll take this too—back
of the man who made a vow
to care for me even unto
calamity, bent over the lawn,
searching for signs of growth.

Epithalamium with Empty Nest

Tonight, in bed, we hear the frogs that just appear
when ditches fill with rain outside our house.
Sounds like a chorus of coffee-counter men

grumbling for a refill. To our ears, at least—to theirs,
who knows, seduction? A way to find another
frog that's crawled through dirt to find himself immersed

in water, darkness, song? I keep thinking of that time
we stepped on a hornets' nest, you carrying the baby
on your back, me orbiting your precious double form.

They rose so angry, embers set on burning holes
into my hands and arms, your neck, but not one
touched the child. Remember? As though some force

protected her from stings—our love? I'm not naïve.
We cleared the railroad tracks, that buried hive, so quick
and swatted off their panicked first defense before

they reached her tender flesh, fat hands and wrists
and cheeks exposed though shadowed under
wide-brimmed baby hat and slicked with SPF-a-million.

Our love, yes. A set of spells we cast each time
we left our little flat. You say maybe our frogs, too,
rise up from underground, not to sting us in their rage,

just to complain, or mate. It goes on all night,
and sometimes I wake thinking it's your breath or the dog
whimpering in sleep, or our kid, though even if she shouted

from her bed I wouldn't hear. She's hundreds of miles away
and five stories up in a city that for all I know is one big
swarm of burning stings. So long we hovered. Swaddled.

Happy to supply our own thin skin for hers. Tonight,
I offer mine, again, to you. When people ask
about her now as though she's died, we check ourselves

all over for the bruise of grief. They don't know how quickly
the strange calm of our days can turn electric, afternoon
into evening, your fingers, your tongue into song.

Not-Quite Empty Nest Elegy
(for my husband, at semester's end)

On the North Carolina to Mississippi leg you call
to talk about Nietzsche's theory of the Übermensch
& next day hit Louisiana & text me a picture
of a dead alligator on the shoulder of the road.
We're trying to connect through these phones

but with every hour you drive of course the space
between us grows. Anyway you're out there & I'm
at home binging vegan jerky & *Felicity*, yearning
to Noel's broad shoulders, his guileless smile,
yearning I'm saying for you & for the past which

all the poets say is basically now so it's the nineties
& pant legs are so fucking wide there could be
anything under there—legs, tree trunks, rain sticks,
anything but guns which back then we didn't worry
about or not so much & we're getting busy signals

on each other's hall phones, don't know where
anybody is, have to wait until the person we want
returns to the last place we're sure they were,
have to scrawl on the door the next place we think
we might go—meet me at the commons, on the quad,

on the roof, in thin air, twenty years ago or
Wednesday when together nearly three decades
we clutched and cried, car running in the drive
& said *You are my very best thing, you are my only thing*
& then because that's not of course quite right

I said *Go get our girl*, you drove away, I went to work,
shooter alert, all clear, drank microwave soup
from a cup at my desk, came home to the dog
in the dark of the house you're not in, not right now,
house we've been together in these past

four months alone, eating tacos every night
if we want to, sleeping naked, naked in the kitchen,
naked holding hands watching TV on the couch
& if I was afraid of losing you in '92 I'm afraid
of losing you now, not your car tipping off that spindly

legged bridge into the bayou, not some pretty
Houston waitress wooing you with cheese dip
& Southern charm, more like you're in the cafeteria
& I'm stuck at the library or you're trying pot
& I'm locked out of my room or you're protesting

Columbus Day & I'm taking back the night
or I'm kissing a frat boy named Chopper
& you're delivering Pizza Hut to stoners.
More like I'm riding the elevator up while you
take the stairs to the basement, not where I

left you, not where I thought you'd be,
or you're back, you're right here, aren't you? Only
something's between us—in the house, on the couch—
it's something beautiful, true, but love, what if
the line's always busy? What if I can't get through?

When We're in Bed and You Take Out
Your Mouth Guard, I Know It's On

Like when, seventeen, I'd slide into your Beetle and you'd head
out of town, summer daylight, and parked among the furrows
of some field, you'd reach for the wool blanket. I knew you'd
maneuver then into the cramped quarters between passenger seat
and glove box, blanket over your head and my lap, where you'd
sweat and sweat until I cried out. Or further back, first winter
of our courtship, nearing curfew, when we'd "watched" *Predator*
again from the Braden's lovers' row, you'd slow to a halt
at the last stop sign before my house. I knew we'd linger there,
under the streetlamp's acid glow, and you'd ask if I *had* to
go home. *Yes,* I'd say, *I better, soon*—but I knew you wouldn't
hit the gas, not for the longest time, three minutes, five,
and snow falling and the silent streets carless, I'd lift my top,
you'd unzip my jeans and treat the expanse of soft skin
between shirt hem and underwear like sex itself, your worshipful
mouth, my whole body lit from within and without. Or even further
back, how I knew by the first electric touch of our fingers
in that dark theater, like a secret handshake—*I know you,*
I need you, like an exchange of life force between two aliens
from planets never before joined across the cold, airless terror
of space, that it was on, that it was on and on and on, forever.

·V·

Multiverse Love Song

for Jennifer

There's a world in which we live on a night bus
between some far-flung high school and our own,
pressed together under a single parka, tethered
each by one earbud to your Walkman while
a stranger drives us through darkness on a highway
that never arrives. And there's a world in which
I marry you and we spend whole lives sharing
one bag of salt and vinegar chips and watching
Mystic Pizza, your fat cat supine on the couch
between us, forever bearing our salty, sour rubs.
And there must be a world, too, in which I never
meet you—my freshman-year mono persists,
my tender spleen excused from the gym class
you must jog through without me. I'm better off,
then, in this world, where the silent miles so often
stretch between us but in which I know keenly
who I'm missing, what song might run the wire,
what belly might bare itself to what hand.

Benediction with Foundlings

Let me cuddle with a dog I don't even know.
—BATHROOM STALL GRAFFITI

Let stray cats trust their matted hides to my hand.
May the next squirrel kit who falls

from tulip poplar to leaf bed curl into the kin-
pink of my palm. May houseflies wobble

from windowsills to rest their black-stitch legs
against my own. Let me hold each iridescent gaze.

And let me lie, somehow so small, upon the ledge
above the porch, where a sparrow often sleeps

through squally dark. When I open the screen door,
she'll fly, shocked by its unoiled cry, into rain.

But if I spoke her language of soft whistles,
offered my breast for batten, my arms,

might she believe at least this stranger,
at least tonight, means no harm?

I Cry Each Time We Say Goodbye Because
I Know I'm Always Sending You to War

You the only one doing the speed limit, the other drivers
seem intent on killing you, their unblinkered swerves and also
the way their carelessness makes you feel: unloved, not just

as a man but as a member of the tribe. They hate the tribe?
That's war. In truth, you feel embattled even when you stay—
one afternoon last spring you napped in the hammock, woke

to a baby jay blinking from the grass, then spotted its wobbly
sibling on the woodpile, testing wings. Though you skipped
dinner, followed the tender pair around the yard till dark,

hissing off the neighbor's cat, that night she mangled both
while we lay sleeping. What comfort can I offer, love,
other than to say we soldier on together? I read a novel

in which two sailors hack the wings off a seabird
and watch it waddle the deck in terror. The scene's invented,
so why do I carry that bird's fear like it's still trapped there

with that crew, their cruelty? What's it mean that I don't
believe in God but I believe in that bird, that the laughter
of those men is real? I think sometimes how terrible

to be a wild creature injured and nowhere to go for help,
no skillful hand to tend your wounds, but then I think of
healing tongues, succor of one warm flank against another.

And of the children who've died, penned at the border,
their parents made to grieve in other cages, locked
by hands. What a world we have been given, love.

What a world we lot have made by hand. Remember
that summer when we drove our car partway up a mountain
so a new friend could cart us to the top in her jeep,

steepest drive to the queendom of her hand-hewn house,
cement floors she'd poured herself and a vegetable garden,
solar panels, rain collecting in barrels? Up there we drank

kava, bitter mud that numbed our tongues, the children
running barefoot in the gathering dusk, then watched
our friend use a shovel to cut the head off a rattlesnake,

just a baby she said, that didn't know better than to belly
into the yard. She threw its body, both halves,
into the fire pit, its mouth still opening and closing

like a slow fist. I'm not saying she was wrong—
villainy is real, but she's no more a villain than
our neighbor's cat. Her nerve awed me, the strength

of her muscled arms, how she could feel sorry for the snake
even while it burned in a hell of her making. As for me,
I feel born on the wrong planet. Or this planet's just wrong.

Here it's always like seeing rabbits at the side of the truck-mad
road—us thrilling at their soft wildness, then dread. This spring,
when fledglings scream themselves hoarse for the morsels

their parents drop into their mouths, I'll usher you inside,
draw the blinds. But come morning, you'll find on the lawn
one body, neck broken, bury it behind the shed.

Poem Written While My Friend Has Bone
Marrow Harvested for Stem Cells

I've learned it's possible to help an injured butterfly by attaching
to its body a replacement wing, that you can return a monarch
to flight by gluing a spare—delicate, particolored thing you have,

in anticipation of this need, collected some spring morning
from the lawn—onto its body, and faced with this astonishment
I'm worried, no I'm grateful, no I'm sad. Like when my mother,

in the impossible blue hour before dawn, wrapped me in a blanket
and carried me to the babysitter's house so she could work
her early shift at the shoe plant or go to nursing school—

me startled awake to unwelcome cold but in her arms in the silent
street, small enough to hold, knowing in minutes she'd settle me
on another woman's couch. I'd have to spend the day in the absence

of my mother. I'd be okay, sure, but for hours I'd stay achy, off
balance. I was loved. Usually attended to. But my need felt
bottomless. Still does, some days. Today. I'm so glad somebody

glues that wing on sometimes. Oftener nobody does, of course,
and those butterflies stay grounded. Must get trampled, eaten,
die in the grass, unfed. But some receive the tender ministration

of hands, precision of kindness—love, I'm talking about love.
That we are this prone to crumple, to tear. That we are subject,
on occasion, to repair. Mended creatures maybe wobble into air,

fly their days sky worthy but imperfect. Achy? I don't know. I'm
happy. I'm worried. I'm sore. Wondering what these hands are for.

Dear Uncle,

I've heard about the chickens, the fourteen cats, each with
a name she scratches in the dry dirt of the yard or the soft
leather of your arms. And the blood clots threatening

in your veins, how—since your brother's Christmas
heart attack—the fear of sudden death keeps you up nights,
stalking the kitchen for handfuls of cereal you swallow

with milk in refrigerator light. I've heard about the pain,
knuckles and knee joints swollen stiff and no way to work
with weak shoulders, sore feet. Uncle, do you remember

the stolen bicycle, midnight hitchhike, the beer you got me
to guzzle by swearing it was ginger ale? You introduced me
to sweet and sour chicken. You introduced me to the sea,

built a swing set for every kid you ever loved, including
me, and that's how I learned that love may wobble on hollow
legs but also it pitches us kicking, reeling into sky. Uncle,

I want to touch down now. Especially since yesterday,
when my mother texted to report you'd called me a miracle,
said those years were hard but I'd brought you joy. I want

to come back to the house where I was a skinny, big-eyed
baby, a singing, dirty faced girl, the house your mother
left, where your father after thirty years chain smoking

and pumping gas to pay the mortgage lost for good
his memory, then his breath. But it's so far, uncle, from here
to where you are, and going home always feels like

traveling through time, like lapsing, frame after frame,
into the past, filmstrip run backward so the flower, twitching,
unblooms, tightens to shoot, then to seed, then to nothing.

Little Deprivation in the Big North Woods

                                  I thought I should tell my sister not to
go there again, never go there,
                                  our grandfather dying
of some disease that makes him have heart attacks
in winter, the thick plastic sheeting over every
                                  window, such meager
light in those rooms and you can't
                    see out, our uncle burning
through his liver and crashing everyone's car, whole family
squatting in that slumped house full of
                                  newspapers and ashtrays,
the ceiling tiles falling, porch steps sinking deeper
every year into the ground, and our brother glowing
with a terrible manic fever
                    or sinking, too, or making
stilted amends or angry we weren't there to nurse him
through the last fever.

                    But I don't say it—don't go
                    home,
                                  and she goes,
makes that northward trudge, past all
Starbucks, all Targets, past interstate highways and also
                                  the hope of ever
distinguishing herself from the soil from which she
                                  sprang
or crawled or never
          fully crawled, and this time Dad
                    tells her two things she calls to tell me.

                    One,
when they were preparing to eat the new potatoes and peas
that are maybe most of the reason
my sister visits at all—that tenderness, that mouthful
                                  of sweet green,

like going home but without the pain, or with a little less
pain—and she was looking for a spoon,
                              my father said *I'll have to wash it.*
There's only one. Your brother
        used the rest to cook his drugs.

                              Two,
a boy of seven,
buttoned into his good shirt, pants ironed, our father let
the music spin him in the center of the school gym,
                              shedding
twelve toothaches and failed scout badges
                              and his father's
unaccountable rage like spare change flung
from his pockets, and then he went home
                              good-tired
and still too buoyant to sleep, so he stood just inside
his bedroom door, listening to his parents
                              in the hallway ask his older
sister *How did he do at his first dance?*
And she said *He looked like a loser,* and that's why,
        our father told my sister,
                              he never danced again.

                  And still I don't say it—never
go home—because what about the front door
always unlocked, damp boxes
                              of rubber dolls and crayoned
drawings, a whole basement full of years
and years and days, same basement where the uncles
working on the cracked foundation found
                              a jar of buried cash, hundreds
of disintegrating dollars some government agency had to
                              microscope together,
send us a check that kept us in
fuel oil and hamburger meat for months.
                              And the photo albums

blooming mold there in the dark—me
bathing in the sink, my sister with her eye patch
in the arms of the mother who left
                              those photographs behind.
What about the few blessed days after snowmelt
when lilac mixes with the scent of mud
                              and you can only think
                                    new, new?
You can only believe we'll be reborn together
                                    somewhere else,
somewhere easier to breathe but the air
                        still smells this
                                    sweet.
What about that money dust—our inheritance
                        finally unearthed—and the way we
                                    dig in, the very ground
                        beneath us a lottery we can't not play?

Sobriety Sonnet

with apologies to my brother, 11 months clean

The boy who cried sunlight, summer rain,
bird-in-the-bush, in the hand, who cried
fiddleheads, brook trout, berries in the field
by the chicken house, again and again ·

who cried lilacs, from each bloom
a hit of nectar and nothing to fear—
he'd pretended for so long the all-clear
while something hungry paced the room

that even when of true wolflessness
he made a bouquet so pretty and perfumed
nobody in her right mind could presume
it wasn't flowers, I called it beast,

saw in the gold-dusted mouth of each bud
a dogtooth sharp enough to draw blood.

·VI·

IV

When I Was Afraid

Maybe I'm five when one day we drive
past an industrial park on the edge
of town, vast flat land behind razor wire
and in the middle distance a fire so hot
it bends the sky, sends up fury after
fury of black smoke, and my mother
tells a joke I don't know is a joke:
if they're not careful that blaze'll light
those propane tanks, which might
explode and take this whole town
down. In that night's dream, my uncles
burn trash they've loose-corralled
in a circle of cinder blocks, grandfather
playing on harmonica a mournful tune
that's really just his deep breaths in and out—
and then the fire leaps its bounds
and settles on the roof, a massive, burning
bird that makes our house into a nest
of flames. Now you. When you're five,
I'll take you to a demonstration
at the fire station, in front of which
they've parked a trailer special made
to emulate a little house, and I'll lead you
through its narrow rooms until the warnings
sound, detector's screech and angry strobe
and wisps of smoke, and we'll escape but not
unscathed. According to the men in helmets,
I'd do best at night to let you cry behind
your bedroom door, shut tight against
what ghosts might try to choke you.
But how could I bring you to this terrifying
place, arm you with nothing but fear,
then take you home and close the door
between us? I'll just vow to be more careful.
Spark no tinder. Give rise to very little heat.

The One in Which I Admit I'm Still Afraid

> What now?
> *Now.*
> —ÉIREANN LORSUNG

Last week you called crying. Someone at the elite
Texas university you attend for free told you
it was too late for you to register to vote
in the midterms. And a week before that you
called crying because Kavanaugh got confirmed.
And a week before that you called crying because
some boy forced his hand down your roommate's
pants and wouldn't hear no. Last night my phone
buzzed with your selfie-with-*I-voted*-sticker,
your wide smile maybe more painful to me
than all those tears. This morning the poet visiting
the school where I teach tells me the president
means to erase the citizenship of thousands
of Americans via executive order, and the poet
who teaches your workshop tells you his cancer
is back. Charles Bernstein writes, "Hold your
own hearings." How? Today, walking, I get a little
lost. The sun is high and bright. The cool air
smells of the sea, but yes, as always, there's this fear.
Beloved child, wise poet, warm body of unstable
energy, I burn. If you told me where to turn, I would.

America You're Breaking

my heart   breaking even my
heartbreak   your stupid
    gleaming bulk calving into darkness
at an ever-increasing rate   My fists
    clench of their own accord   the word
no always vibrating   my mouth
    I've had a headache for one thousand
ninety-one days   America, beloved
    does every kid pretend to be dead
doing the dead man's float?
    Is everyone comforted knowing
there are creatures in the Marianas Trench
    10,000 miles down   creatures nobody's
ever seen   nobody ever will?
    Does everyone think as much as
I do about whales giving birth
    in the sea   those massive
babies borne from saline
    into saline   Sweet abiding
underwater milk   America, I was
    a stranger and you teargassed me?
I was your daughter and you grabbed
    my ass   your son and you shot me
in the street   I was a baby and you
    taught me to stand on the toilet
hiding my feet?   America,
    darling   imagine the quiet
of the sunken city   no panic room no
    closet lollies   no ricochet   just that dumb
undulation   that senseless sun-lashed glow

Poem Written the Day Before the Pandemic Brings
Our Kid Home from Europe Unexpectedly

Some fired, some fired-up man murdered, some man again murdered
coworkers in the bottling plant today

and my daughter is in Portugal, where the air, she says, smells good, a little
like Florida—oranges, hibiscus, and the sea

and we know he'll do it again, not him, he's dead, among the dead in the
bottling plant, among the bodies carried from that place, I'm saying some
man will do it again, we know this

and Annabelle is in a restaurant in Portugal, where patron after patron rises
to sing Fado full-throated in the grotto of dim light by the bar

and I have never left this country, my mother has never left this country, my
grandfather left only for war, never will again, he's dead, ate sardines and
ketchup in a chair that was also his bed, watched Westerns till the TV turned
to one a.m. static, rose at four to pump the gas of folks on their way to work
or to Canada or who knows, who knows where some of those people wound
up, but he stayed here, stayed at the pump until lung cancer, smelled of
kerosene even in his casket, I know, I put my nose to his rough dead cheek

and in a courtyard in Portugal my kid eats danish while a peacock spreads
his ridiculous shimmering scrim of tailfeathers, a show meant this morning
only for the modest peahen the diners also ignore in a clattering of forks
and conversation

and we will each of us have to get out of a body somehow

and first we will some of us see all of Lisbon rolled out from the yellow
pinnacle of a castle, we will some of us eat petals of ice cream hand scooped
and pressed into the shape of a bloom, ice cream blooming from the
sugar cone, too beautiful to eat, but some of us will eat it, the way today
Annabelle does, knowing we can never, outside of Portugal, taste such a
thing in this life.

Elegy in Quarantine

This month I've been sad enough to watch
    about a hundred hours of home renovation on TV,
        just to see something clean and neat nailed over
    something ugly. But in one episode the demo man
huffed hot cat box smell from an uncovered fireplace
    then climbed to the attic and startled cluster
        after cluster of bats with his flashlight beam.
    Reader, he hated them, flexing their gray velvet
wings, unfurling in the sudden glare like lovers
    scared apart or babies woken from a nap.
        He meant to call an exterminator, but I
    consoled myself with what I knew—they're protected,
have to be rehomed. At forty-five I sometimes feel
    a way—desperate and achy—that makes me
        think or sometimes say *I want my mother.*
    There were six hundred bats in that attic,
and if I'm honest I don't trust the folks
    who sucked them into cages, don't know
        if they're scattered like scraps or curled together
in a complex of clean pine boxes, waiting for a dusk
they'll navigate by song, fill their bellies then slip back
    to the silk of bodies strange to me, yes, and terrifying
        to the demo man. I've so often felt myself
    scrapped, that whoever's job *I* was
left the job undone, but when I remember love, my mother
    loving me, one thing that comes to mind is a night
        when my ear ached like an awl pounded in,
    like bone cracking so near the brain to think
was pain, and we didn't own a heating pad, didn't own
    so many things, so she warmed a dry washcloth
        on top of the toaster and held it to my ear
    while I cried, and each time the cloth cooled
she went to the kitchen to heat it. Those moments
    without her and the compress—which didn't make
        the pain go away, I don't even know

if its piercing diminished—may have been
      my first bereft moments, but Reader, she kept
coming back to hold that comfort to my throbbing
and my fear, so a rhythm kicked up that night
    and lasted maybe forever, me alone and then
      rehomed, sorrow in both states, yes,
   and the strangeness of my body, made to suffer,
and the bodies that give me succor, how we furl and unfurl.

General Absolution

In some ways so glorious is the world I forget
how terrible it is—leaning over a ditch of purple
weeds and runoff, alive with pulsing frogs
the size of fingertips, the flutter of their tiny
throats, the pinpricks of their black and shiny
eyes, their skin a green that's somehow tenderer
than pink, I think, *This is enough to have come here for.*
Today I sat in a bath so hot I said *fuck*
as I sank and, sweating and stinging, drank
a glass of ice water, chewed every cube,
though if I crack my teeth I can't afford
to have them fixed. Bliss, bliss and forgetting,
and between sips I read a book about 9/11,
learned that when the first tower collapsed,
a man running from the wave of debris begged
a fire department chaplain for forgiveness,
and the chaplain said he'd offered general
absolution the moment the building started
to fall—*general absolution*, all souls granted
mercy in an instant—the cops, the accountants,
the jumpers, the hijackers, straight to heaven,
made clean. Will you know what I mean if I say
we should have designated all the water
holy? I'm trying to forgive you. And if you're
wondering who you are, you're everyone.

Acknowledgments

I WOULD LIKE TO thank the editors of the following journals in which these poems (or earlier versions of them) first appeared: the Academy of American Poets Poem-a-Day series ("When We're in Bed and You Take Out Your Mouth Guard, I Know It's On"); *Adroit Journal* ("Poet Loves Hunter Though She'll Eat No Meat"); *Asheville Poetry Review* ("Dear Uncle,"); *Baltimore Review* ("The Parting"); *Bear Review* ("But Nothing Bad Ever Happened to Me in the Woods"); *Crab Creek Review* ("Poem Written While My Friend Has Bone Marrow Harvested for Stem Cells"); *Four Way Review* ("Epithalamium with Paper Bell"; "Sobriety Sonnet"); *Los Angeles Review* ("When She Speaks of the Fire"); *Mom Egg Review* ("Poem Written the Day Before the Pandemic Brings Our Kid Home from Europe Unexpectedly"); *Nelle* ("I'll Tell You What Helped"); *New England Review* ("I Want to Tell You What Poverty Gave Me—"); *POETRY* ("Little Deprivation in the Big North Woods"); Poetry Daily reprint/feature ("I Want to Tell You What Poverty Gave Me—"); *Poetry Northwest* ("Thrownness"); *Rupture* ("Lo"; "Elegy in Quarantine"; "General Absolution"); *Shenandoah* ("Epithalamium with Empty Nest"); *Shore* ("I Cry Each Time We Say Goodbye Because I Know I'm Always Sending You to War"; "America You're Breaking"); *Sugar House Review* ("When I Was Afraid" [appears in Part I. in this collection]; "Often in Dreams She Was My Girlfriend Until I Remembered, Still Asleep, That It Wasn't Okay"); *Thrush* ("Epithalamium with Inventory"); *Tupelo Quarterly* ("Benediction with Foundlings"; "The Self Says, I Am"); *Water Stone Review* ("Lessons").

I owe enormous thanks to friends of mine who also managed to be friends to so many of these poems, by handling them gently and offering insights that helped me find their final versions. Anna Lena Phillips Bell, Ashley Hudson, Malena Mörling, Sophia Stid, and Jessica Jacobs—this book owes much to the sharpness of your minds and the generosity of your hearts.

And to Meg Day, *Lo*'s first reader—passing this thing between us made it and me better in ways for which I may never find words. For the luck of you in my life, I'm profoundly grateful.

I tell everyone that working in a building full of artists makes the days brighter and the writing easier. It's true! For making me feel accompanied on the long journey and for cheering me up and on, I owe huge thanks to my colleagues and students in Kenan Hall.

Annabelle—you make me braver, and that makes everything better.

Finally, Mark, my beloved—everybody knows the *speaker's husband* is deeply and beautifully good, that he's patient and kind, that he's wise and funny and handsome, and, baby, he can't hold a candle to you. I'll never stop feeling a little bad for everyone who doesn't get to be your best friend. I'll never stop thanking you.

Notes

The title and epigraph of "The Self Says, I Am," along with some italicized phrases in the body of the poem, come from Theodore Roethke's "What Can I Tell My Bones?," copyright © 1957 by Theodore Roethke. From *Collected Poems* by Theodore Roethke, copyright © 1966, renewed 1994 by Beatrice Lushington. Used by permission of Doubleday, an imprint of the Knopf Doubleday Publishing Group, a division of Penguin Random House LLC. All rights reserved.

The epigraph of "Monachopsis Aubade" comes from "Ich bin auf der Welt..." ("I'm too alone in the world...") by Rainer Maria Rilke. From *Rilke's Book of Hours: Love Poems to God* by Rainer Maria Rilke, translated by Anita Barrows and Joanna Macy, translation copyright © 1996 by Anita Barrows and Joanna Macy. Used by permission of Riverhead, an imprint of Penguin Publishing Group, a division of Penguin Random House LLC. All rights reserved.

"When She Speaks of the Fire" takes its title and epigraph from Katie Ford's "The Fire," from *Blood Lyrics*, copyright © 2014 by Katie Ford. Reprinted with the permission of The Permissions Company, LLC on behalf of Graywolf Press, Minneapolis, Minnesota, www.graywolfpress.org.

"The Parting" takes its epigraph from Jane Kenyon's "Having it Out with Melancholy," from *Collected Poems*, copyright © 2005 by The Estate of Jane Kenyon. Reprinted with the permission of The Permissions Company, LLC on behalf of Graywolf Press, Minneapolis, Minnesota, graywolfpress.org.

I borrow the notion of "the parting" as a Japanese translation of "goodbye" from Meg Wolitzer's *Surrender, Dorothy*.

I make liberal use of a Louisiana crematory's authorization agreement in "After Not Having Spoken to His Father for Fifteen Years, He Authorizes the Cremation," which is almost—but not quite—a found poem.

The epigraph of "Not-Quite Empty Nest Elegy" comes from Terry Gross's 2008 interview with W. S. Merwin.

Iowa Poetry Prize and
Edwin Ford Piper Poetry Award Winners

1987
Elton Glaser, *Tropical Depressions*
Michael Pettit, *Cardinal Points*

1988
Bill Knott, *Outremer*
Mary Ruefle, *The Adamant*

1989
Conrad Hilberry, *Sorting the Smoke*
Terese Svoboda, *Laughing Africa*

1990
Philip Dacey, *Night Shift at the Crucifix Factory*
Lynda Hull, *Star Ledger*

1991
Greg Pape, *Sunflower Facing the Sun*
Walter Pavlich, *Running near the End of the World*

1992
Lola Haskins, *Hunger*
Katherine Soniat, *A Shared Life*

1993
Tom Andrews, *The Hemophiliac's Motorcycle*
Michael Heffernan, *Love's Answer*
John Wood, *In Primary Light*

1994
James McKean, *Tree of Heaven*
Bin Ramke, *Massacre of the Innocents*
Ed Roberson, *Voices Cast Out to Talk Us In*

1995
Ralph Burns, *Swamp Candles*
Maureen Seaton, *Furious Cooking*

1996
Pamela Alexander, *Inland*
Gary Gildner, *The Bunker in the Parsley Fields*
John Wood, *The Gates of the Elect Kingdom*

1997
Brendan Galvin, *Hotel Malabar*
Leslie Ullman, *Slow Work through Sand*

1998
Kathleen Peirce, *The Oval Hour*
Bin Ramke, *Wake*
Cole Swensen, *Try*

1999
Larissa Szporluk, *Isolato*
Liz Waldner, *A Point Is That Which Has No Part*

2000
Mary Leader, *The Penultimate Suitor*

2001
Joanna Goodman, *Trace of One*
Karen Volkman, *Spar*

2002
Lesle Lewis, *Small Boat*
Peter Jay Shippy, *Thieves' Latin*

2003
Michele Glazer, *Aggregate of Disturbances*
Dainis Hazners, *(some of) The Adventures of Carlyle, My Imaginary Friend*

2004
Megan Johnson, *The Waiting*
Susan Wheeler, *Ledger*

2005

Emily Rosko, *Raw Goods Inventory*

Joshua Marie Wilkinson, *Lug Your Careless Body out of the Careful Dusk*

2006

Elizabeth Hughey, *Sunday Houses the Sunday House*

Sarah Vap, *American Spikenard*

2008

Andrew Michael Roberts, *something has to happen next*

Zach Savich, *Full Catastrophe Living*

2009

Samuel Amadon, *Like a Sea*

Molly Brodak, *A Little Middle of the Night*

2010

Julie Hanson, *Unbeknownst*

L. S. Klatt, *Cloud of Ink*

2011

Joseph Campana, *Natural Selections*

Kerri Webster, *Grand & Arsenal*

2012

Stephanie Pippin, *The Messenger*

2013

Eric Linsker, *La Far*

Alexandria Peary, *Control Bird Alt Delete*

2014

JoEllen Kwiatek, *Study for Necessity*

2015

John Blair, *Playful Song Called Beautiful*

Lindsay Tigue, *System of Ghosts*

2016

Adam Giannelli, *Tremulous Hinge*

Timothy Daniel Welch, *Odd Bloom Seen from Space*

2017
Alicia Mountain, *High Ground Coward*
Lisa Wells, *The Fix*

2018
Cassie Donish, *The Year of the Femme*
Rob Schlegel, *In the Tree Where the Double Sex Sleeps*

2019
William Fargason, *Love Song to the Demon-Possessed Pigs of Gadara*
Jennifer Habel, *The Book of Jane*

2020
Emily Pittinos, *The Last Unkillable Thing*
Felicia Zamora, *I Always Carry My Bones*

2021
Emily Pérez, *What Flies Want*

2022
Melissa Crowe, *Lo*
Maggie Queeney, *In Kind*